9780310769903
I0531407

"There are lots of stories in the Bible, but all the stories are telling one Big Story. The Story of how God loves his children and comes to rescue them. It takes the whole Bible to tell this Story. And at the center of the Story, there is a baby. Every Story in the Bible whispers his name ... " —JSB

The days leading up to Christmas are called "Advent." *Advent* means "coming." It means God's Great Rescuer is coming!

As we wait for the Rescuer to come, as we wait for Christmas, we'll go on a journey together. This collection was created for this special advent experience. We'll read a passage of Scripture each day of the Advent season, think about how God loves us, and tell the story of God's rescue plan. The plan that began even before the creation of the world and leads us right up to Christmas day.

Press the musical note button to hear a Christmas carol or a reading from *The Jesus Storybook Bible.*

HE'S HERE!

The Nativity, from Luke 1–2

Everything was ready. The moment God had been waiting for was here at last! God was coming to help his people, just as he promised in the beginning.

But how would he come? What would he be like? What would he do?

Mountains would have bowed down. Seas would have roared. Trees would have clapped their hands. But the earth held its breath. As silent as snow falling, he came in.

And when no one was looking, in the darkness, he came.

There was a young girl who was engaged to a man named Joseph. (Joseph was the great-great-great-great-great-grandson of King David.)

One morning, this girl was minding her own business when, suddenly, a great warrior of light appeared—right there, in her bedroom. He was Gabriel and he was an angel, a special messenger from heaven.

When she saw the tall, shining man standing there, Mary was frightened.

"You don't need to be scared," Gabriel said. "God is very happy with you!"

Mary looked around to see if perhaps he was talking to someone else.

"Mary," Gabriel said, and he laughed with such gladness that Mary's eyes filled with sudden tears.

"Mary, you're going to have a baby. A little boy. You will call him Jesus. He is God's own Son. He's the One! He's the Rescuer!"

The God who flung planets into space and kept them whirling around and around, the God who made the universe with just a word, the one who could do anything at all—was making himself small. And coming down … as a baby.

Wait. God was sending a baby to rescue the world?

"But it's too wonderful!" Mary said and felt her heart beating hard. "How can it be true?"

"Is anything too wonderful for God?" Gabriel asked.

So Mary trusted God more than what her eyes could see. And she believed. "I am God's servant," she said. "Whatever God says, I will do."

Sure enough, it was just as the angel had said. Nine months later, Mary was almost ready to have her baby. Now, Mary and Joseph had to take a trip to Bethlehem, the town King David was from. But when they reached the little town, they found every room was full. Every bed was taken.

"Go away!" the innkeepers told them. "There isn't any place for you."

Where would they stay? Soon, Mary's baby would come. They couldn't find anywhere except an old, tumbledown stable. So they stayed where the cows and the donkeys and the horses stayed.